GERARD WOODWARD is a prize-winning writer of poetry, short stories and a number of novels, including an acclaimed trilogy comprising *August* (shortlisted for the 2001 Whitbread First Novel Award), *I'll Go to Bed at Noon* (shortlisted for the 2004 Man Booker Prize) and *A Curious Earth*. He was born in London in 1961. He is Professor of Creative Writing at Bath Spa University.

Gerard Woodward

The Vulture

PICADOR

First published 2022 by Picador
an imprint of Pan Macmillan
6 Briset Street, London EC1M 5NR
EU representative: Macmillan Publishers Ireland Ltd, 1st Floor,
The Liffey Trust Centre, 117–126 Sheriff Street Upper, Dublin 1 DO1 YC43
Associated companies throughout the world
www.panmacmillan.com

ISBN 978-1-5290-2770-9

Printed and bound by CPI Group (UK) Ltd, Croydon, CR0 4YY

Visit **www.picador.com** to read more about all our books
and to buy them. You will also find features, author interviews and
news of any author events, and you can sign up for e-newsletters
so that you're always first to hear about our new releases.

For Suzanne

Contents

The Vulture

In the dead grass, at the foot of the cliff
By the blackthorn tree, I lifted the head
Of the vulture that had been watching us
For so many turns of the moon I couldn't remember.
And as I lifted him his wings fell open and wide
As if to embrace me, and he was like a woman
In an evening dress, at a premiere, or an opera,
Though his legs hung like a hanged man's,
And his U-bend neck seemed to struggle and gulp.
I carried him back to the village, one wing
Hanging low so it dragged in the dust.
Why had he died? they asked me, when they saw
His body so perfect, undamaged, the eyes
Still open, the tongue still wet. I could only suppose
He had come down to feed, and something
Had troubled him. There was no blood
On his bald head. And when we cut his belly open
Later, we found nothing in there
But the usual, unspeakable things.

Captives

Two nestlings came down the chimney.
Brothers in buttoned-up shirts of black,
With arrows for faces.
They had the stance of hostages,
Hands tied behind backs, swaying slightly
In their breathing, their hearts moved them.
They questioned silently, puzzled
By their new circumstance, their surprise
Plummet through chimney blackness
To land on the upside of the flue seal,
Then the second surprise
When we unscrewed the slatted vent
To provide an escape downwards. It must
Have cast a beam of golden light
Into the gloom from which they'd dropped.
It was an hour or more before they
Summoned the nerve to fall through
The narrow slot into the fireplace below.

They said nothing in the whole time we knew them,
Apart from the one cry of shock after that
First fall, their voices mingled with the leaf-like
Crash and bounce of their fletched bodies
On the wooden panel. Then, when in the hearth
Itself, they stuck together in a corner,
Their plumage heavy with ash, almost invisible
Against the scorch marks of the old bricks.

Silence. They passed no comment,
Gave nothing away. They would accept
Anything as normal, but not this,
They knew they were in a place
They didn't belong, that they'd washed
Up on the wrong shore,
Where everything presented itself
As an apogee of its kind.

I thought of the bathtub aviaries
My mother made, filled with leafy
Boughs, hopeful for the torn thrushes
She brought in from the wilderness,
Of the chopped worms she fed to them,
The water she eyedroppered
Into their overspilling beaks,
And of the evening songs that filled
The human space in the hours
Before they died.

A flaw had thrown
These two into our lives.
Self-gagged, they stayed silent.
We didn't ask to be their captors.
Before they died,
They would have told us
Anything we wanted to know.

Hornets

for Paul Evans

Hornets at night,
broken-backed
and tan-eyed,
rising and falling,
rising and falling,
sounding the depth
of a cottage wall.
They are night-time
animals, bringing
their poisoned cup
to the same dark table
as moth and bat.
They butt the pearl
of the outside light
to shift the littler,
barely visible flies
that cluster there,
that fall sideways
to the limewash.
The hornets follow
and pick them
like grapes harvested
on a new planet.
Under the light of its one
pearl moon, they move,
and remember.

[4]

Wasps

Every hour or so another one makes it,
Coming up through the hole in the floor
Where the hot water pipe rises to the radiator.
It is like the scene in *The Great Escape*
When the prisoners emerge
A few yards short of the forest.
Here a last hurdle of glass
Holds them back from the free world,
Unless I'm here to let them out,
Pinching them between the pages
Of whatever I'm reading.

All the warm autumn it has been like this. And all summer
They have been our open secret, since the day
Of the risen-again queens, when one, searching
Our walls, found a way in. The rest was history.
We feared our closer neighbours might petition us
To have them killed, waiting for the tentative knock,
The concerned enquiries. They are *our* wasps!
In the end, from their high castle, they did no harm.

Now, I watch their fall. I can't think
How they've suffered, just that their
One-by-one exits are like the slow beat
Of the autumnal clock. In their yellow
Sameness they might be rolling off
A production line, the faded starlets

Ejected through a night club's fire door.
Bankers whose gold has fallen through the floor.

In mid-December, when the last one has gone,
I try to rework their long march backwards,
Down under the floorboards
Into those strewn galleries I've never seen
That leads up through the chimney
To the void above my study
And there I see what they've lost
The infinity of empty rooms, the cold
Engine of an empire – desiccated, unsweet Alhambra
That had once overflowed with kindness.

Starfish

A single instance of the physical world
Can account for the whole of someone's life.
This man, for instance, who collected starfish,
Lifting them from the floors of shallow seas —
Brittle star, fragile star, asteroidea
Who lay on their backs, open-armed,
Wanton, idle. He carried them away
And laid them to dry under a yellow sun,
On the volcanic sands of Ascension Island,
One star pouring its light on another.
And then he did it again, and again
Sailing from island to island to island
Until his empty life was filled
With a silent crowd waving, waving.

The Fish Head

I found a fish head
With the face of Elizabeth the First
Blue blood clotted in its neck

The same look of disdain, or disgust
Or disbelief. As unloved
As anything I've ever seen.

I was in between two football pitches
In an empty playing field.
In the distance were houses,

Tiny and red like Monopoly houses.
The pitches were pricked with studmarks,
The only trace of some likely nil-nil draw.

There was other litter —
A can of Heineken, a juice carton,
A polystyrene tray faecal with

Curry sauce — in all this the fish head
Shone like a silver brooch, though it stank
And bled, still, onto my hand.

I looked up, and for the first time
Saw the common crowd,
A thousand, maybe more,

Seagulls circling in a great wheel
That seemed to hang like the roof
Of a cathedral over our suburb

Each bird playing its part as though
Toiling to move some massive structure,
Or haul in the Earth as their own catch.

Or they were watching as one eye,
A single lens focused on the severed head
I had in my hand, that one of them had found

On a shoreline, and had dropped here
Thirty miles inland. Suddenly I had them all
On a string, their centre of gravity,

Their Sagittarius A,
Daring me to put the thing down
And just walk away.

Story of the Thirsty Bee

This is the story about bees that I tell
Whenever there is an awkward silence
To fill, or when I have carelessly answered
The door to peddlers of a new religion – that once,
During the first great drought of this century
When the whole of Somerset was shrunk
To the size of a human tongue,
I found a bee that had lost its mind,

Like a traveller wiped out with travelling,
She had thrown off her luggage and
Was resolved to do nothing but sit
(If bees sit), and become a pinpoint of stillness.
The desert formed around her, pulling all greenery
Into its sands, the dunes spread from the bee centre,
Outwards in concentric waves, until I realised what had happened
To the bee. That in the whole county there was not
Enough water to fill her little gut.
She was dying of thirst.

I scooped her from underneath on a timetable,
Lifted her to my level, peered into her tackwork face.

Having no other means of giving her water
I let form on my lips a globe of saliva which fell
In a cloying bundle onto the sheet beside her.
As if a lamp had been switched on by her bed

The bee stirred for the first time, moved towards
The water source, unrolled the straw of her tongue
And sucked. I felt a dance of triumph in my body
That I had not only diagnosed the bee's condition,
But I had found a practical solution.
I was almost embarrassed at how long the bee spent
Supping my spit, like when you expect a peck
On the cheek from a party guest
And get French kissed instead. Ten minutes, thirty
Minutes, an hour she spent filling her body, my single drop an
    overflowing
Fountain in her heart. Unable to watch any longer,
I found a shaded spot and rested the bee there
Left her still drinking, solitary and silent, like all the best drinkers.

And in the hour I walked in deadly heat and thought
About the bee and how I, like a well-intentioned missionary
Might have infected a whole tribe, that the bee might carry
My impurities back to the hive, and from there to other hives,
And the entire world population of bees collapse.
And then later I saw us through a bistro window
Sitting together at a table flagrantly, sharing a dish of sugar
As though neither of us was married. You haven't thought
This through, I said. Your children will never forgive you.
Realising too late that I had spoken the words aloud,
My wife, who was by my side, had heard enough
And was by my side no longer.

It rained that night, as I lay naked on the garden bed,
I took its cold stings as a just punishment for my life.

Dynamism of a Dog on a Leash

I am the dog; no, the dog is himself, and I am
the dog – O! the dog is me, and I am myself
Shakespeare, *The Two Gentlemen of Verona II:iii*

A man walking a dog becomes a single creature
That is neither wholly dog nor man, a centaur
Whose two halves are connected by a thread,
A planet and its moon orbiting a common lead.

How many dogs are at the end of this leash?
How many paws tread? How many tails lash?
The dog overlaps itself, a self-overlapping lap
Dog, back and forth through time it leaps.

A man walking a dog is a thing of two halves
And when the dog shakes it has a dozen selves,
Thumbs through the cards of itself, a Rolodex,
Or dictionary of the dog turning through its codex.

The leash is taut, then loose, then tight, vibrates
To the tune of the dog as he pulls ahead, then retreats,
He is caught in the breeze of his own world-infatuation
Like a kite that is fixed to the ground, or harpoon

Launched at some pavement-whale, when the leash is extended,
Uncoils from its box like an astronaut's umbilicus, or thread
To follow to the exit of the labyrinth, recording his movement
Above, below and through the many fixtures of a pavement.

Man brain. Dog brain. Like the tin can telephones
They find a connection here, so it can be anyone's
Guess who is leading who through this wonderland of kerbs.
This is the thought that most delights, that most disturbs.

The Garden In Late Autumn

The Garden is in tragic mode
Shaking her bottle of pills,
They spill. She glazes over slowly.
The birds are sick of her.

Why has no one cleared up this mess?
We don't talk to each other.
The brilliant albums have been locked away,
Or worse, torn to pieces.

You want to visit, but the ground
Seems uncertain. Should she be left?
But what's this? A butterfly feeding
On stale nectar. Or is she dreaming?

Walking My Dolphin Down Whitehall

I am walking my dolphin down Whitehall.
He swims into the red vault of a telephone box
And poses to have his picture taken
The receiver to his ear, as if making a call.
People are amazed that he even has ears
Before they think how he can handle a phone.
Children think he is a balloon,
Until he opens his mouth.

There has been a demonstration,
Its angry litter still hangs in the air.
Whitehall remains closed to traffic
Though the demonstrators – men in black
With shaved heads – have taken to its pubs.
All down Whitehall they drink – in The Silver Cross
The Lord Moon, The Clarence. They are like
Cab drivers, or van drivers, or paparazzi.
I don't understand their London English
As I walk my dolphin past them.

And my dolphin, on his ribbon of leash,
Dives in and out of them, curves round them,
Overleaps and air-splashes them, as though
The sea is men, men in black, a black sea
Of shaved heads, waves of hate, crashing.
I have never seen anything like it
One of them says. A reclining bulldog

In a Union Jack coat fills his arms,
Like the roast beef of old England.
My dolphin swims right past his sticky flews.
The dog snaps hopelessly at his slipstream.
Tourists, nervous of the men in black,
Pet my dolphin, can't believe he is wet,
That he can sigh real salt water from his blowhole.
It is like touching the other side of the world
I hear them say. My dolphin smiles, clicks, leaps.

Whitehall is drunk and closed to traffic.
If I didn't look at them, I'd think the great
Windows were boarded up, that the drains
Were overflowing, the statues broken
Or missing down to their ankles.
Someone murmurs that I should send my dolphin
Back to the sea where he belongs,
That I am cruel and don't understand the needs
Of cetaceans. But he is my dolphin,
I tell them. And this is the sea.

Cows and Cricketers

The cows are all in profile,
And facing left, as though they had been sketched
Onto the field by a child. They are
The colour of gingerbread, and when
They turn their heads towards us,
We almost expect them to have big
Happy faces, but they have the usual
Cow faces, that chew, and seem indifferent.

By a freak of perspective, the cricketers
In the next field have been reduced
To the size of white mice, and are playing
Their match on the backs of the cows.
It is like a very English infestation, the wickets
Like hairs sticking up from the cow's shoulders,
A spin bowler starts by the tail and runs up
The spine and hoists the pinhead ball so it
Vanishes into a monstrous twitching ear.

Cows and cricketers each have a special
Relationship with grass – to one it is a food
Source, something they seek to contain
And to digest. To the other it is a kind of surface
Whose texture and saturation can affect the movement
Of a ball. Something that would make no sense at all to a cow.
As if in illustration of this fact, I saw one beast
Swallow an entire outfield in one go, then move on
Lick by luscious lick, to the batsmen, and the slips
And the wicket keeper, all gone.

What is an Animal?

for Phoebe

We fell ill at the zoo
Giving in to a weakness
As the gorillas floated
From their thrones of straw
Or climbed their knotted lines of hemp.
We were sick among the tamarinds
Who had raided doll versions
Of our grandmothers' wardrobes,
Antic in their marmalade stoles.

And we had so wanted to see the animals.
But they warped in our tears as we tried
To hold the bile in our mouths,
And we had to make do with looking
At each other instead, at our
Bicycle saddle snouts, our mountainous
Shells, our bodies folded and layered
Like lettuce. We wanted to see you, we said.

By now the zoo was closed and no one had found us.
At night the animals came to us with keys in their hands.

The Eight Fields I Pass Through
Walking the Dog

The fields are the baize-lined drawers
Taken from the old writing desk

Though some are convex and others slope,
They are all defined, and fit against each other.

They rarely contain animals, apart from humans
And dogs, and these only temporarily.

The main crop is grass, uniform and ordinary,
Though in two fields it grows wild and with flowers,

Meadows that you might see maids with parasols
Meander through, or swing above, on the tree swing.

In late summer the whole impressionist array
Is folded into tight plastic bales as smooth as ganache.

In another, maize is sometimes grown, rising
Faster than hotels, providing endless corridors

In parallel, doors facing each other from which green
Daggers are thrust. When harvested, it feels as though

A city has been stolen overnight.
Then past the allotments and their delicate sheds

To the last field, where weak horses stand like toys,
Their backs turned on mounds of damp hay,

As though they have gone on hunger strike to save
Their field from the fate that has befallen the next,

Where the new houses stand fresh and still empty,
Watching hungrily through the broken hedge.

The Piano Stool

Black wood, as though the piano had calved.
Four straight legs, thin and unmuscled,
And a long handle each side of the seat.
The seat itself, upholstered in something like
The pelt of a black cat's neck, lately worn
To a hard, tarmac glaze, except at the edges,
Where the fur bulged treacle-thick.
It opened like a musical box, though its music
Was in printed form, a library of sonatas
Stored as if for incubation, stacked flat,
A dozen or so deep, a well that I could never fathom.
Sometimes, when there were too many for dinner,
It would be carried through and set at the dining table,
A black sheep among the regular chairs,
A too-high perch for whoever was put there.
Still with its secret cache, it stood awkwardly,
Looking as if it might cry out for its mother,
Massive and immovable in the next room.

The Piano Tuner's Cough

The tuner of our piano is making his final call,
And I am here to watch him work. His jacket's
Off and hanging from a chair. His sleeves
Are rolled like two white life-rings round each arm,
And in this way he strikes me as a working man –
A gardener come to tackle our wilderness,
A plumber trying to sort our drainage out.
He plays one note, then turns the tuning pin.
The piano is opened up, its strings exposed,
As if prepared for surgery, or strapped
To a chair, gagged or drugged or blacked out
Or fully conscious but with shredded nerves,
Like my mother at the dentist when her last few teeth
Were pulled, half cut with drink that made it
All the worse when her china-thin and sooted
Lower incisors snapped. He plays one note –
A half-truth, a near-truth, another turn and then
Another turn. He listens. The voice comes back
To him, barely a whisper. Telling him something
He already knows.

We are getting on okay. The tuner stands
My company, though looking back I see him
As a man in pain, ill at ease with kids.
His strongest wish is that I'd take my leave
And toddle off to my world of shrunken heads.
But he gives my questions their tired due and speaks

As if to someone older than myself
Which is a sort of compliment, but I
Do not understand a thing he says
And in between my questions are long rests
(Of a semibreve at least), in which I feel
No awkwardness and turn my ear instead
To the piano's slowly rising pleas for mercy.

The piano tuner coughs and from his mouth
A piece of silver jumps and lands on a spot
Of lacquered black just inches from my eyes,
To settle there a moment – barely a moment –
Before the tuner wipes the thing away
With the same soft cloth that gloves his tuning lever.
It is like a trick in which he's disappeared,
Leaving just a memory in his place
Though I still see the bubbled thing he'd wiped,
As if he'd coughed it straight into my thoughts –
awkwardness made visible; a little
Palace of the solecism, domed
And chambered, mirror-walled; pavilion
At an international exhibition;
Intersecting geodes; a jewel of
Buckminsterfullerene; shortlived hothouse
Seeded with more versions of himself,
His hereditary stuff, badge of how
Animal he really was, poor man.

Now I wonder if he was a father
With little angels seated at a different

Keyboard, generous with his time, loving,
Kind, but then that structure comes to mind,
The one he coughed, and through its curving glass
I see him as a tyrant who would rather
Cut his children's fingers off than hear them
Play a wayward note. Dr Harmonious,
Is he ill? Has he an ague?
Why this sudden vulnerability?
Is he sick of this tuning game,
And in his dreams sees armies of
Pianos with their bass strings drawn,
And elaborates his grand designs to turn them
Into other things? A reassembled
Fleet of sleek black galleons, for instance,
Their strings restrung as rigging. Or renailed
As garden sheds in which a quieter life
Can be pursued, seedlings raised in silence,
Noiseless pots of peaty soils tuned
By sunlight. Or might he snap completely
And take an axe to the reverberating wood
And find the other instrument I'm told
Is hidden there, that if you chopped away
The surrounding pine the structure that emerged
Would be something very like a harp
(It happens in a Marx Brothers film, I can't
Remember which one), as though it stored
The equipment for an afterlife, though some
Blackness in him sees his soul instead
Arrayed on red hot strings and hammered at
By hammers of burning lead. Tuner in torment.

No more false notes, no more half-truths,
The piano cries out in pain as he reaches
For its tongue and pulls it out, again.

A black cloud. A thunderhead. A stilted
Land. At two or three, a world above.
Its underneath to me seemed like a map
Of roads in an ideal city, intersections
And junctions of black wood that my Matchbox cars
Could drive like they were in another land,
Suspended, antipodean – and whose feet are those,
In the upright world, treading so lightly, cautiously,
On the brass pedals, the same soft tread
My father's suede foot applied to the brake.
Then my mother, open-toed, overdoing the sostenuto.
At four or five another country came
Into view when I could see above the dark
Horizon – ploughed fields, but ploughed with a blade
Of pure exactness, and intersecting at
An angle – making overlapping slender
X's in three dimensions. An ocean,
An inland sea with waves unreally parallel
That turn their tides on golden breakwaters,
And come ashore on beaches of green baize
And a hundred capstans round which each string is moored.
The hump-backed bridges to nowhere, the dampers like molars
Chewing at the sound; in the bass more like incisors,
White felt v's that bite into the vibration
And silence it; the little gold leaf bunkers
Like a pharaoh's coffin that has been opened up

And found to be full of the ashes of burnt-out Woodbines.
The music rest with its black fret sunrise, the half moon
Rinks where cigarettes sometimes stood on end
In the place where a metronome once kept order. Time
Is not a tuner's concern, he plays the notes
Without a thought for a regular beat,
A musician from a universe that hasn't begun
Though with his keys turning and tightening
He can seem like a winder of clocks, just as he
Can seem anything— The priests who stopped
For sherry and a chat in those times
When our house was a place that could be visited,
The Provident man, the man who delivered our food.

It was his final call. He didn't come again.
And now the instrument is dying.
It is a wounded thing – don't let its size
Fool you, it is weak, lame, battle-scarred.
It is infected, it has rot rising from its golden feet,
I had thought he had come here to cure it but instead
He has given it an illness. This bronchial man
Is sick, there is something tapping at his heart,
Plucking at his own decaying strings. Perhaps he died.

And the piano lived on like an orphan in a fallen city,
A child whose frozen cot can't hold its warmth,
Whose voice drifts further and further from its human note.
You wouldn't treat an animal like that.

An observation blister on a futuristic craft,
The tuner within, peering out into a galaxy gone dark,
In mourning for his dying trade that once survived
On an instrument in every house. He had never seen
A grand like this, sitting in a room done up in white
(Lino, walls and ceiling) the Bechstein of such polished
Black it was like a hole in time. He'd known it then,
Before its world fell in, with a gifted young musician
At its seat, and he could see perhaps the things
It had in store, and maybe this is what had made him sick.

Our Furniture

They were the nearest we had to a serving class,
Took our coats and our weight,
Held dishes of food for us to eat,
Played music for us, protected us,
Became shields and took whatever was thrown at them.
On quiet evenings or long Sunday afternoons
They would let us torture them, get under their nails
Carve into them, slit them, dance on their heads.

And still they helped us, supporting our backs
Offering us shoulders to lean on, they gulped
Down our clothes, withdrew into themselves
Swung themselves shut, even changed
Their form entirely for the children – became
Horses, bulls, hills, corrals.
When sick, they treated us.

Some pieces were haunted, others nailed in,
Filled alcoves like walled-in priests or nuns.
Woodenly loyal, they would carry on
Even when worn out, would even
Keep working after they had died,
Long after, if we would let them,
If there was anything left of them.
There was nothing
That could stop them being what they were.

They passed no judgements, made no comments
Instead they bore our traces, scars of their own,
Aware that without us, all they could do
Would be to stand still, and stand still for ever
Until their glue decayed, until their nails and screws
Rusted in the atmosphere, in the humidity of doing nothing.
And then in some distant future they might
Succumb to the hoards that lived within them.

The Sink

When the house was demolished, they found a stone sink
Beneath the rubble, shining, white and intact as a pearl,
Made of stronger stuff than the house to which it had belonged.

They'd taken everything else – the pan tiles and castellated pots,
The marmalade cakey bricks. Was there value in this thing as
    well?
Someone laughed at the thought, said sinks like this were slum-
    goods,

Where women scrubbed babies until they bled, then left them
To drown while they sank their gin. No one wanted them now.
Another took offence, said he'd had a sink like this when young

That he would fill to the brim and set sail a newspaper navy
To re-enact the Battle of the Nile, then bombard it with lighted
    matches.
Another proposed that the sink might be made of solid marble

Hand carved into its present form, from a block that had once
Comprised the left foot of Michelangelo's other statue of David.
Someone else said that in a square by the church of St Adjutor

He had seen a fountain playing from a sink like this. Starlings
Bathed there, and when they flew, the fathers on benches
Thought for a moment it was raining, and didn't mind.

Tommy Noddy

Guest sprite, pinned to the ceiling,
Your dazzling anatomy writhing there
Asking to be named, and we point
And name you – that you have a name!

Pocket galaxy, incandescent gnat-
Cloud, nest of vipers, force-field
From a black and white sci-fi flick
Life without substance, the mind-possessing

Consciousness-eclipsing energy,
Pure thought, the daydreaming
Of sunlight, the sugar lions who've
Come to the water hole.

You are seen more rarely now,
Where sinks full of water are less
A thing. You have been locked
Away in an age of appliances

Where the rivers run through microducts
And high speed drums, you never now jump
That frightening height to jiggle your luminous
Intestine to say – I am here! I am here!

Ivy Anxiety

Wrong to worry about this thing
Alive on the other side of the wall
That through a kind of neighbourly
Negligence has outgrown someone
Else's domain and reached into mine,
Though not quite into it, not yet.
I think of the house on the other side
Of the town, that is a sort of Jack-
In-the-Green, dressed from head to toe,
In a thick and delicious coat of leaves.
No architecture visible — chimney,
Window, gable, sill, they are all gone,
What's left is a blue door, deep within
A living porch. But no number. No name.

The Obelisk

In the wake of the most recent crisis
They would take a drive to the obelisk

Have their lunch there, where the monument stood
On the·far side of a cornfield, at the edge of a wood.

It seemed like the right thing to do, a place to go
When there was no seaside near, no archipelago

Of favourite islands, just this piece of farmland
On the edge of the borough, an old estate, still husbanded.

Solid stone, yet it seemed lighter than the trees
That formed its backdrop, a slender human trace

That almost disappears, its massiveness easily lost
For a moment's concentration. It was like a ghost.

A memorial, though they didn't know it, to a child
Who'd died in infancy, the reason why the estate was sold

And the woods were left to run wild. It was always a surprise
An hour or two later, when they'd taken the slow returning drive

Back to the city, to find it was just as they remembered
The houses cold and unburnt, the bodies undismembered.

We Are Alicia and Jane Clarke

We are twins and we are under the trees.
She dresses in blue, I dress in salmon pink.
I sit on a chair someone has put out.
Do you think we look alike?
Does our colour coding help you tell us apart?
Do you think we should just be called Miss Pink and Miss Blue?
Alicia is blue. I am pink.
We've brought our hats out here with us
With their brims wide as cymbals, or planetary rings.
Why do we have the same hats?
We are a puzzle. She holds the flowering baby branch
Of a tree that touches the sky. It is like the little
Sister of the bigger tree.
There is difference there.
Our skirts are lovely convex curves of silk.
We are like little bells that you could pick up
And ring to summon one of us.
Which one?
Ignore my sister. She is an ape.
There are two of us in this universe
How do you figure that? I've rested
My hat on the stump of a tree.
I'm me. I'm me.

The church is enormous.
The church is nothing. It was lost
In the Somerset mangroves.
My sister is an Orang Utang.
We were discovered by the first
West Country missionaries. I could fold you
Into my silk like a beaten egg into flour.
Are you cross with me? She's cross with me.
The leaves of the ash are reticulate.
Too leafy. Too leafy. What am I sitting on?
My dress has swallowed a chair. It has
Consumed all the furniture of the world
In fact. It is sunset. Or it is dawn?
I can no longer tell which is which.

The Meeting

The floor of the quarry is as level as a nave.
Spare, stunted birches grow in thickets,
And in the encompassing cliffs other trees,
Misshapen, fork from cracks.

Someone has set out chairs in a circle
As though for an important meeting.
They are ordinary dining chairs, the sort
You used to find in waiting rooms,
Or round the tables of rarely visited uncles.

But they are damp. On the upholstered seats
Of some, thin lawns have grown, from seeds
That must have fallen there.
Each blade of grass points upwards
Like a nail in a bed of nails.

You wait like a sitting tenant
In the last bedsit on Earth,
For the procession to arrive
And for the chairs to be filled.

Carpeting

The floors posed a different problem.
The winter wind came up between the boards,
And set the white rug to flap like a skate's wing.
They laid a fitted carpet, which gave nowhere for the rug
To go but on top, white on white, but still it would not die.
A ruck appeared, transversely, and reappeared
Soon after every straightening, like the smooth bore
The builds and builds but never reaches the shore.

It reminded her of her grandfather's house,
How his living room had a carpet that was deepening
Shades of blue, with fish swimming, woven
So convincingly that going in there it seemed
The old man was afloat in his armchair,
And that she had walked across an ocean to visit him.

Morgan's Mantelpiece

At birth, give every man his own mantelpiece,
For him to sit at the foot of, thinking – what next?

And then to carry round with him
For the rest of his life, from one home

To the next; Tonbridge, Tunbridge Wells,
Weybridge, West Hackhurst, King's.

A spiritual alcove, a place for the less loved,
And if your new room has no fireplace,

Still you will nail your mantelpiece above
The space where it would have been.

Mine was not like yours, no Tuscan gravitas.
Fluted legs, not columns exactly, in white

That supported two shelves, but with enough
Character to make me feel the shock

Of its absence when one day it wasn't there.
I oversaw the task of bringing it in

From the cold, my father and my brother
Taking one upended leg each, hauling

The dead body (probably stuffed with tenners
Someone joked – the woodwork that had

Faced the wall unpainted chilled
With its rawness), then up the stairs

To its new resting place, my bedroom,
Where it lived, unattached, just propped

Against the wall, or on the floor, upside down.
I claimed it had been a friend, when asked,

Indulging a childish sentimentality,
That I held conversations with the Mantelpiece

That it had a human name, though when pressed
could only come up with 'Fred'. And a surname?

'Henry.' 'Henry?' '-son' 'Fred Henryson?'
Though in my room, I was troubled

By the mantelpiece's firm, blank silence,
Not reticence or coyness, just the empty

Gape of brainlessness. A triumphal arch
Commemorating nothing. The fire

That should have burned was cold wall.
It was itself burned, in the end, I think

In an extravagant bonfire. What turn in me could
Have put my friend to the flames?

I had outgrown that shelf
And it was time to know what next.

The Plot

Already we were on the fifth draft of the garden
Scratching each season out and feeding it to the next one,
The pages sank without trace, but were still there,
Deeper than could be read, only remembered. The first
Year, when the seeds wouldn't come off the soil
But stayed there, like buttons fastened to the black
Cardigan of the earth. Then, as if from nowhere
A line of celery, that later outgrew itself and flowered.
The rest were deleted by the slugs and snails,
Who had a gift for that sort of thing.

Page after page the plot refused to thicken.
In the damp summers it could feel as if we were stranded
On an island that had been eaten bare, and that unless
We could dose the soil with life then the land
Would be taken back – by giants, perhaps.

Potatoes were our first success, detonating quietly
In the depths, giving the garden its first definitions,
A structure and form that was a green proof of our authorship,
Not the random flowering of some birdcast seed,

Then courgettes, far more than we could eat
That seemed to grow in a single day – shiny, smooth
Necks of fruit glossy as cricket balls. Sweetcorn made its own
Brief forest, radishes blushed in their shallow pit.

The whole page was written in one summer.
But already there are black notes in the margins.
A new editor is in charge. Old lines have been dug up
And no one is sure what to write next.

Pieces of String

Hillwards, shadow herds
                   leap
the dry
  stone walls,
      thin as pieces of string, from here. A man
        kitesurfs
            the bald face
    of the beach, his plough of puff
                   carving
          up the sky,
            but what starved
      furrows he
  leaves
      in the sand. The sea
        shuffles
        its cellophane-fresh,
            laminated deck,
          waits
        till I'm not
looking,
then
slides
        a picture card under my feet. The gravestones
      turn
      their names and dates inland,
          blank slates in the quaker cemetery
        face

the ocean's back. A woman
                examines
her daughter's eye
        easing
        the furred lids apart,
    looking
for the grain of sand
                she said
        was there.
        But there is only the world
of her eyeball.
        In the fairy glen a mothers' circle
            hangs
            knitted wildlife
        from young sycamores —
            a nest of woollen goldfinches,
                a crocheted
        jellyfish. The man with the birdwatcher's
            telescope on his shoulder is not
                    recognised
            as human by the dog who
takes
        him for a horned
            or trunked creature. The man's mother
        explains
        this as he
            falls
to his knees in
        worship.
The jellyfish

dry
their soft clocks
on the pebbled shore.
Each is a planet that has
lost
its vibe or
a brain that has
become
a
piece
of
string.

The New Seasons

Adwinter, when there is warmth in bare forests,
And snow is promised but never comes, and certain
Incorrigible leaves retain their colour,
And the clouds are dumb and cannot rain
And the sills are thick with demolition dust.
It lasts until Christmas and a little beyond

And shakes hands with Epiwinter
In those unmarked days when the year turns,
Characterized by a sense of doubt and uncertainty,
About whether the year should have begun at all,
And what year it is anyway, and who you are.

Beespring is a season of three days or three weeks
When the ancients awaken and begin
Rebuilding what they had lost in another age,
Searching our houses for what was theirs,
Finding the scrolls and maps hidden in lofts.
They read the hieroglyphic texts carved into fence posts
And the treads of wooden step ladders.

Persummer, when the stars begin to fall,
And the birds in flight are struck by sudden
Gravity, opens with the first brush
Of a forgotten comet's tail and the licensing
Of avian slaughter, when the Perseids
Nail the trees to the ground and the shooting

Parties bray at the harvest moon. Cancer spills
Into the roots of the leaves, and the polls
Show growing support for parties of indifference.

Snow

Can seem generous. Giving you more of itself
Than you want. More than you could ever need,
Sitting in your heavens like a reassuring thatch.
Making everything in the garden look brainy.

I open the front door to find another front door
In negative, as pale as a horse, the outside
Turned inwards on itself. In fact I can pass
Through its thin crepe without touching it.

The town has run to fat, we can barely squeeze
Into its parks. Trees and beds are bloated.
You'd think the tobogganists did this every year
Instead of finding a little corner of their memory

To work with, saddling the next generation into their
Bucking, skeletal frames, demanding that they
Remember this moment for ever. The rest of us
Are deskilled, even of walking, and learn instead

A kind of flightless bird waddle that sees us to the shops
That have run dry of bread and milk.
We didn't realise how much we depended on those
Two things. Those two white things. Odd.

Frog Deaths

The frogs in the pond have read deep
Into their history. Scholarly, they hold
Seminars, conferences. Their writing
Comes to life, bubblejets of print,
Clusters of it. Oh — they have wired together
An artificial brain! Now they sit back and rest
Up to their necks in the common culture.
They have their own gardens of grey fruit.

So little confidence. They treat me
Like lightning, are gone the moment
I flicker at the back door, leaving their
Handiwork for me to find, their sums
And workings out, scattered papers,
They've gone deep, too deep.

In the freeze they all died
Trapped beneath the ice
Having gone too deep for too long.
They'd known it as a hardening
Of their thoughts, their jelly ideas
Had resolved into something solid
That they couldn't get through,
They beat their brains on white
Cots and cradles
But nothing was given in answer.

Freezing

Moving things marry
To form non-moving things.
Hardness arrives like a single feather,
Carried on the skin of the stream,
Then a log jam of feathers
Staunching a seaway. Or

Diamonds that appear from nowhere,
That fill out and touch each other
Point to point, like a sky
With too many kites.
Where did all the kites come from?

The knight picks out his armour
From the dark, empty wardrobe,
Slots together gauntlet and vambrace
But the joints are rusted, he squeaks
At the elbow and knee.
Cries out for oil in the cornfield.

Daylight arrives in the form
Of cubes and tiles that I fit together
In a kind of collaboration.
I have got the feel of things,
Look at my face, just two tiny holes
And a perforated rose for a mouth.
My hands fuse to my gloves
My gloves fuse together
My blood forms a queue at the border.

She Dances With Horses

Unequal in weight,
She leans against him
As if against a wall, her back
Touches his mahogany shoulder.
She stretches an arm across
His acreages of ribs, then sweeps
Around him, turning on points,
Her human body working lightly,
Finding the unnatural beauty of movement.
She seems as weightless as a moth,
Though the horse, when he moves
Seems weightless as well.

He stops. The woman returns to him,
Leans against him again, then bends
And lifts his front leg by the fetlock,
Draws it out, extends it, he allows her.
Later, when he moves, it seems
He is coasting through a language
Newly garnered, that a dialogue
Of blood and bone has been formed
Though we, an audience, can only take
On trust the fact that he is not reliving
Some primal fear, troubled by a thing
Not found in his ancestral strain –
A human ballerina. When he dips
His neck it is as though he thinks

She might bear a tail that stings
Or have teeth other than those she displays
That could bite into his glossy flank.
Or maybe this is really something
That is like an enormous flower
Caught in the human breeze of being.

She says she has found a doorway
Into that veined and velvet head,
Though we wonder how she knows
That he doesn't drag this new tongue
Behind him like a plough.

Plans for an Ideal City

(several maquettes)

I.

I take our set of wooden steps
And saw them into pieces; pull nails
From the gills of an empty cupboard
And hammer them home elsewhere.
I cut through batons, find triangular
Offcuts
    Pin and tack them.

                  A pillar. A plaza.
A flight of steps rising to the left
To the right – walkways, a ramp, a spiral

Footpath.

I lift the world
To my eyes, check sight lines,
See people walking from all directions
Past a mural of interlinking ovals
Thinking they're not lost.

2.

I've spliced a coffee cup and made a pavilion,
Covered a ping pong ball in silver foil
And stuck it on the end of a pencil —
A public park, an observation tower.

Balsa wood boulevards. Scalpel and glue.
Sunlight falling in the wrong direction.

Architects — they know what it's like
To be giants, to look down on the

3.

Houses made of a single block of wood,
No windows, no interiority, just the wooden rooms,
With wooden air,
And the concert hall —
Orchestras within solid balsa.

That grand varnished canal suggests
A lowland capital, somewhere in the Walloon.
Which is sculpture, which is house?

4.

Built in the form of a pentangle
Eight straight roads lead to your octagonal palace
The fields of lettuce and kale
Radiate in all directions — O I will
Eat nothing but wander gardens
Picking fruit, on your roofs
Are whole words or worlds. A desert. An oasis

5. *Machine City*

A cat would pick apart
What you have here, and this one, roughly made, you have
Seen together what you once had, put it together again
Circular city, concentric roads linking circular pools
Perfect transport

Though you have made this world into something less

Easily lived in — where is this city, all I see are
Fields, fields and a road
A road and a small stadium
A pylon, a flying machine,
A public park, a tree.

6. *Radiant City*

The city is only visible at a distance
But this city only comes into being
When lifted to the eye

The model city becomes the thing itself
The model city is not a city, but an object
A city is not an object but a space in which
Objects have relations,

Even though you have moved up these narrow
Black roads you have not seen them from the outside

To see the city from the outside, to be beyond it
Over it and above it. I am easily lived in
I draw the red oxygen in through my tarry veins

I am a floating city that is built on clouds,
I heave my buildings onto vapours,
I have been thought through, like the walled cities
The diamond shaped, or quatrefoiled cities,
A city in the shape of a heart or a brain
A city that thinks.

7. *Veganopolis*

Its road plan is based on the roman cauliflower
The rivers flow with juice, and are a main
Form of transport. On the cow-shaped barges
Musicians alternately play and ply.

By the red fountains, mothers feed.

The Mountain

We lived on the plains,
Our chimneys were the highest things
For miles around. The far off hill,
Like a heart murmur on the horizon's
Otherwise flat line, drew little of our attention.
Something that was always there,
But under another jurisdiction,
That we might visit one day
If our lives ever became empty enough.
We hardly thought about it,
Nor could pick it out even on a day's walk
Back from school, or chasing the puppies
Across the onion fields where there was
Nothing else to look at, until someone said
Look at the hill. We'd never noticed before
How it had detail, a craggy shape, with cols
And cliffs, that it was notched and ravined.
Later we realised it was in our own county,
Just an afternoon's drive away
That there were cool pine forests on its lower
Slopes. And soon it attracted clouds.
You could forecast the day's weather
By glancing at the hill, to see if it had its hat
Of cumulus or its skirt of haze. Visitors came
From other counties, envious of our hill.
*We didn't know you had a mountain so close
To your town, you're so lucky*. We fashioned

New lores and sayings, warned travellers
Of climate anomalies, how it can be sunny
In the town while a blizzard weaves
Its deadly tapestry on the summit.
What were those white patches?
Snowy reaches. A glacier. The new hotels came.
Ski shops opened, a chair lift was built,
Its rotary dumbness a new rhythm for the town.
We were right at the foot of the mountain,
Had been all our lives. Indeed, our outer suburbs
Were built a little up its side. How could we have
Not known? Those steep streets
Were the sloping neighbourhoods
Of the wealthy who enjoyed views out across
The town they had always lived in.
Nothing mattered for them
But their laddered gardens.
I moved out there myself, never dreamed
I'd spend my retirement as a man
Of the mountain. The town itself
Has become impossible to live in.
Always in shadow, the waters
Of a hundred rills flow constantly
Into the new rivers and fill them.
The town floods time after time.
Crops and gardens are washed out.
Everyone has gone.
Even the good houses are starting to slide,
We've had to strike out, climb upwards,
Overcome our vertigo and pull at the winberries

To get higher. You've forgotten
There was ever a town down below.
All you can think about is how to keep warm,
How to find food, thinking always that the answer
Lies at the summit, though you doubt
If you've the strength to get there now.
People coming back down who failed
The climb say they haven't got the right
Equipment. What do I need? you call.
Oxygen, they say. You need oxygen.

A Bowl of Lemons in Lemon County

Their silent, motionless wrestling,
As if each is trying to suppress
The secret of its own yellowness
And pushes others into greenness,
Or greyness. That they have flesh,
Seeds, juice seems unimportant –
They put everything into their colour.
They *are* their colour. Some
Have almost lost it, glimpsed
In the curved apertures,
In the recesses and niches –
Black pubic triangles where the light
Fails and colour is crushed into memory.
The lemons you'll never see,
Deep among other lemons.
How do they manage such joules
And not move, or be giant?
Why do they not argue? Clean
Little planets, blue in the night time
On the coast of Amalfi where
They can be eaten straight from the tree
Like plums. Temptation, to reach out and touch,
Or tip the bowl and watch them rush
Away from each other, fissile material
Pouring out of a discrete singularity.
If I could take each and juggle with them,

A dozen at once, inflationary and self-
Perpetuating, a solid state. Yellowness
Moving in spotlights across my emptiness.
They have so much to give. I can only half
Understand that memory I have, of a tender
Who, thinking himself unobserved, gorged
On a quarter of this raw fruit, and afterwards
Shook as if skewered, his body
Filling with sudden sharp certainties.

A Judgement

You married a woman then divorced her.
You then married that same woman's daughter.
Your first wife was a bridesmaid at your wedding.
She was maid of honour to her own daughter.
Your ex-wife was also your mother-in-law.
She lived with you both, alongside yours
And her children from previous marriages.
You had three children by this woman.
This added to a total of thirteen children
In the household, though many were by now
Grown up. They still lived with you, some
With their own partners, who moved in with you.
There is evidence that they loved you.
It was not a big house, yet you managed.
Even when your grandchildren were born
You found room in the house for them.
You ruled over this domain like a top dog,
Sniffing the air for trouble and loyalty.
We may never know the reason things changed
But at some point the relationship
Between you all broke down. Perhaps
It was the conversion of the loft,
Or maybe it was the loss of the allotment,
But you hardened, and all of you hardened.
It was as though, in your words, you had all
Been laminated. You took the children
Out of school and tried to educate them

Yourself, but, too late, you realised
You knew nothing. You bought a telescope
To teach them the stars, but you could see
Nothing through it. The hardening continued
Until, in your words, you were like pieces of Lego.
The kin and not kin, friends and lovers.
Your repeated beating of your head
As you sit in the dock, your elaborate displays
Of grief and remorse when you curl up like
A paperclip have not convinced the jury
And they have not convinced me. They are
Tiresome displays of playacting and show how,
Even now, you see yourself as the victim in all of this.
Those pretty children were full of hope
And were entitled to enjoy the full span of their lives.
You are a disappointed man, but not because of this.
Your disappointment goes back to the years
That were lost – we don't know when.
You are an absurd individual. Foolhardy
And harebrained. There is only one judgement
And one sentence that can be passed down to you.
You will have it soon, and then we will be done with you.

Ordinary Time

Nothing is awake
Except in the way it is always awake.
We count the days as moments of light,
Unmitigated except by cirrus or scarves
Caught on an updraft. They are the empty
Boxes the recycling vans leave for us to fill.
The days in lieu, leap days, days of prose,
When ink is the dark companion,
Walking you back to your door.
The moon leafs through its directory
From C to D. Nothing works
Except in the way it always works.
The pigeons bed down under the bridge,
Dogs waltz on the long-abandoned band stand.

The Third Expedition

after Ray Bradbury

I sailed the red canal to my grandma's home
And found a tailor's dummy in her place
Though still she spoke and made me pinch her skin
To prove that she was real. I touched her face.

Her rocking chair looked out across the plain
Where human prints had yet to make their mark.
Are you my boy? she said when we had supped.
I spat a pip and waited for the dark.

She said, out there the people come and go
Like memories of a place we thought we knew.
The pink and level sands stretched far away
And then I began to see the people too.

The dead. Ancient friends. The long lost mas and pas.
Like nothing we'd ever seen before on Mars.

A Tour of the Neighbourhood

This great rock is where the Robinsons' House once stood.
The rock fell out of the sky, square onto their bungalow,
About a million years ago. To our surprise
The Robinsons and their descendants continued
Living beneath the rock, unknown to the rest of us,
And slowly, over the millennia, they hollowed it out
From below, and eventually carved windows
To the let the light in, and a doorway so that they
Could come and go. They filled the windows with glass
And the door with wood. They dressed the outside
So that it looked like pebbledash and tiles
And so the rock gained the appearance it has today
Of a perfectly ordinary, rather uninteresting bungalow.

The Phases of Twilight

Astronomical

Now, in the back room of the universe
Someone switches off the light
Just as here a light is switched on
In the flat of the early riser.
Look out of the window and you wouldn't know
That in the superstore the shelves are beginning to fill
Or that in the hidden power stations
Furnaces are widening their smiles.

Nautical

They are closing down the stars
Not just singly, but in clusters,
Whole districts are lost at a turn,
Galaxies fall into deepest indigo.
There are enough left to steer a ship
Into port, too few to leave port again.
The last shop window
Of the night is smashed.
In petrol stations mannequins
Stand guard over buckets of sand.
The whole of a lorry's energy
Drains into the earth.
In underground tanks the work
Of starlight is stored and meted out.

Civil

Daylight in all but name.
Only Venus survives, and she is
Slowly burning up like an old
Halogen. A forest in the east
Is inflating with light,
Looks like it will burst any moment.

Sunrise

The Cars at Daybreak

The cars are in their comas of frost
They don't remember anything —

How to start, how to release their locks.
With others I nurse their bandaged eyes,

One I see is chipping away
At a quarter light like a sculptor.

We are creative, are we not?
Mine seems bound to its ice like a new skin,

I have to hack, use the sharp edge
To get under, then suddenly it rips apart,

I'm tearing the pages of my car's mindlessness,
Like pulling the sheet from the mock-

Ghost to find another sheeted figure beneath.
Car, think back, don't let the gorgeousness

Of this white flock fool you, even when the
Liquid crystal of your intelligence has faded.

Oh — there is someone in there,
Sitting with the patience of a baby mammoth

Defrosting in the car's gaining warmth.
That together we must carry somewhere.

Somme

    The towns have perfected
A certain way of remembering.

We have discovered a board game
      that tests our knowledge of European languages.
Its batteries are sticky with vinegar.

The staircase
    is an oak tree's troubling dream.
  Climbing it we hear the stir
of a disrupted tongue,
      find furniture like buildings
a wardrobe with battlements.

    In the garden, swallows test the emptiness
Of disused barns, and we fail

To nail the sound of a beehive
    To an actual thing.

At night homage is made
To the gods of thunder.

    Floodlit ball trap.

In the morning we breakfast like children on bread and jam.

Three Garages

Three garages. Two side by side,
The third, small as a daughter
At right angles to the other two.
Blue wooden doors with frosted
Glass panels at the top. Never opened.
Nothing ever came out of the garages,
Or was put inside them. They may have
Contained anything, or nothing.
We don't know who they belonged to,
Who used them, what they were for.
We felt they should have been ours,
Because they were beside our house.
Between our house and the garages
Was a space so narrow I could only
Enter it as a child, sideways, to retrieve
The balding, grey tennis balls
That regularly fell into the gap.
Sometimes I would climb
Onto their corrugated roof
To rescue another, tentatively,
On all fours, across the giving
Asbestos. We could have done
So much with the garages – studios,
A warehouse, a place
Where my dreams for an all-
Encompassing railway layout
Comprising an entire national park

Could be realized. Find out who owns
The garages, my mother would say,
See if you can lease them, rent them,
Buy them, even. They should be our garages
They are almost part of us.
Instead they stayed as they were, like
A family numbed by years into stasis
Unable to move. Then my father
Stepping back from some work on the gutter
Fell through, and so they contained him.

Hailstorm, Boulder

A jackpot of ice

Tat tatting, tat, tat, tat

Pure, white musketry

On the hood. My Ford Taurus
Is a tin can in tin pan alley

Someone gone mad with a hole punch
Done the whole day with it

Pray for the windshield
Reinforcements, extra fire power

The lovely chaos bounce of them,
Broadcast, sowing the ground with coldness.

My Eyes

The optician shows me pictures
Of the insides of my eyes.

An aerial view of two deserts
Side by side, with a dried

Riverbed and its tributaries
Branching, rebranching inwards

To a knot over the blindspot.
I'm almost ashamed of my beauty.

We are like a couple glowing
Over a scan of our own unborn.

It is as though she has taken me to
The back door of her house,

Or my house, or both our houses
At once. Do you have a key?

She says. No. Do you?
She says, If I took your retina

Onto my fingertip, it would look
Like the peeled skin of a garlic clove.

[73]

She takes me into orbit
Around the planet Mars. Those dried

Watercourses – all the tears you've shed
In your life wouldn't flood this little plain.

Shall we go there for a holiday?
We plan a route together, mark out

Camping spots, where to pitch a tent
Among the rods and cones.

With her pencil torch she has lit
The cave where light already wipes its feet.

She has written something on its walls.
Do you have the key? Yes, this is the key.

Glasses

Once, I tried on your glasses,
And in the concentrated liquor
Of the world they displayed —
Smaller than the real one, but
Neater — I felt beyond the reach
Of myself, as though I had tunnelled
Through the everyday, and was looking
Back down its shaft to a coin
On which you were heads, I was tails.

Coming back, readjusting to my own
Sight, the slanting walls slowly
Straightened themselves, and then
I saw you putting your glasses back on
And your face slowly falling into position.

Eating Habits

I should really stop eating with the very old
And let them have their meals in peace,
Remove myself from the garden centres
And try instead to find a garden of my own.
I should steer clear of hospital cafes, and refrain
From taking my tea with the drip-fed,
Reject the thrill of feeling unnoticed
By those who have stopped noticing things.
I am going to stop making trouble just for the sake
Of a cheap eat, stop snatching sweet silence
From the mouths of people who really need it.
I must learn my place and stop picking blackcurrants
In cemeteries, or making gin out of graveyard sloes,
Now, while there is still some space between us.

The Corridor

Here is the machine – about the size
Of a food processor, padlocked to a desk
In the corridor behind the reception area
With its little army of standing robots.

It has a short tube, just wide enough to take
Your arm. When you sit there, schoolroom-
Stiff and straight backed, you can put it through
All the way past the elbow, which rests on a nook beyond.

You have taken an arm wrestler's stance,
Though your opponent has already thrown in the towel.
Press a button and nothing happens,
For a moment, and then the lining of the tube

Begins to thicken, the machine takes in a long
Continuous breath, then holds it.
Numbers on a digital display scroll upwards
Speculatively, as though a problem in mathematics

Is being thought through, and you are thankful this is not the day
The machine goes mad and carries on counting for ever.
Otherwise, it has you where it wants you,
In its grip, like a lonely grandparent.

At the end of a long corridor there is a room full of pain
Too far away to be felt from here. Now there is just
Tightness, almost too much. And then a long withdrawing
Sigh, and numbers, like thoughts of water, falling away.

To My Extracted Tooth

So you won't be with me after all
When the day comes, now that you've gone

Like a child too old for its room
Dressed still in your silly tinsel hat.

For a while you were my golden quinquereme
Docked by my tongue's unstable jetty

Gently unloading your cargo of pain.
Was it something I said? Something I ate?

(More likely.) I feel your absence with my tongue
The satin of an empty bed, still warm,

Still bloody – it was where you were born.
The day you went is the closest

I've come to being beheaded. After all
We did for you, rebuilt you from the foundations up

Like a terrace after the Blitz, with a valuable
New roof. Did you think you were too good for me?

It did feel, at times, as though someone
Had secretly planted a tree in my garden

That gave endless golden apples
But I didn't know they were apples of spite.

All the same, I wish you'd stayed.
Your fall took me by surprise, it was as though

Drug gangs had come from the North
And stripped your life down to bare walls

And left you with nothing to sit on.
I have you now in an envelope meant for a child

That I feel I must post somewhere
If I can remember an address.

The Window

i.m. RLW

In this least holy of places I found a temple
That you had a hand in building. A Homebase
Stood on the other side of the roundabout,
Three hundred parking spaces were laid out
Across what must have been fields or waste-
Ground that summer when your monumental

Window was lifted into position and, with due
Ceremony, unveiled to admit the bread and butter
Light of Chichester. Then a mayoral address,
A photographer from the national press,
A lunch and after – sherry with an undertaker.
It was something you had always wanted to do.

The building was sixties council house gothic,
Orange brickwork and a whitewash portico.
The ground level windows were standard PVC
With net curtains behind, the sort you see
In cul de sacs of corporation bungalows.
It could have been a surgery or wellbeing clinic

Though here they burn the bodies of the dead.
How did it ever become the norm
To scorch beyond all chance of resurrection
The corpses of our loved ones? The beautiful fiction

Of the dead waking from their yawning graves is gone
In a plume of industrial smoke. It's rather sad.

Nearby, a garden had been planted,
One that couldn't have been there when you
Attended the inauguration of your soaring glass.
Someone in a polo shirt was watering the grass
Widowers sat in silent contemplation of the view,
Or perhaps they were enchanted

By your window with its doves in flight,
Swarming towards an irresistible star
(Apt for a place where people are burned)
I wonder how many of those left behind have turned
To see the light coming through your engraved fire
And felt their hearts move into the bright

Shadows of your window's brilliant mansion.
It almost makes us want to weep – or laugh –
That it has survived for so long and not
Been vandalized, boarded up, demolished or put
To some other use, and that your life
Has had this glorious and indefinite extension.

We might feel pity that it is only seen by those
Who never really wanted to be here,
And that they will forever link your flock
With a sense of loss, though maybe the trick
Is to see those doves as a different kind of fire
That lights an unremitting darkness. Who knows?

Chinoiserie

Because it was there, in the kitchen – levels
Of willow patterned china reaching upwards
Like a cliff or a fall of blue scree, so high I might
Expect to climb through different strata of my
Own ancestry and find my grandfather sitting at the top
Like a doll suddenly wide awake and frightened
Of heights – I climbed. Or I expressed a desire to climb
Or I imagined myself on the palisades of my old
Grandmother's scullery, where the cups hung
Like hollowed flints on brass hooks. I didn't expect
This from you, I might have said to the woman
I never knew, on whose treasured dresser I was perched,
All this chinoiserie. It's like you've constructed
Another country in vertical levels to sit at right
Angles to your own mid-Welshness. Climb through
My porcelain, she might have replied. And each plate
Reveals its sameness, the temples, the dancing
Swallows, the chapel-in-a-boat, catkins. Did you
Have an oriental cousin, someone who'd
Travelled out east? Did you even have a dresser
Or willow patterns plates to fill it with?
And I climb as if on Cadair's slopes, away
From the path, falling upwards through time
And looking down, watching the fragments
Of blue crockery rolling towards the lake.

Paraffin

The petrol station opposite St John the Divine's
Under a canopy of light while the church towered
Darkly above. Two pumps for petrol and one
To the side, behind a partition, for paraffin.

She was the woman we visited, my father and I,
On winter nights, sometimes in snow, so that I
Would hold onto the back of his long, brown
Overcoat, to ski behind him in my school shoes.

One hand holding the empty can, light
As a basket of paper chains. A plastic tube
In the waist of the machine, then a coin in the slot
For the pink stuff to gush and fill the can. I would

Take the weight of it but only for so long.
It was my father's burden to carry back,
Which he did – I now like to think – a little furtively,
The transaction mechanical and faceless,

The looming church with its pyramid of green copper,
Overseeing everything. A gallon of warmth
Hanging from my father's hand,
As if we had stolen fire from the gods.

Sunflowers and Dogs

The last sunflowers of the century
Are growing on the allotment.
Raised poles on which leaves are strung
Like big, generous names, and faces
As big as our own, their manes
(Marred, married) raggedly
Beautiful, each a collar of light.
They grow with such speed it's like
They've been nailed through from below
To pin sunlight to its bed.
With age they grow slack, layered,
Nodding among floppy green tutus
Or the coarse chiffons of dowager
Petticoats. And where have the dogs
Come from? What are they doing here?
In the garden of human absence they seem
To accept these dry giants
As their masters. See how they cower
And shy, as if shouted at, as if voice
Came from the fibonacci faces.
They daren't even piss
But curl their spiral tails and lift
Their ripped purse ears to hear
What they might be commanded next.

Shanghai

The Pain

She walks as if she has a pain
In the small of her back. She rests
Her hands there, in the lumbar region
As if guarding her vertebrae against theft,
Carries herself like someone walking on ice
Or on a staircase that isn't there.
At the entrance to the hospital her father
Uses a walking frame for the first time.
Dressed in his night clothes he stands still
In the flow of daytime people, like the captain
Of a little boat at anchor, or a farmer
Driving the most fragile of ploughs,
That has come up against something solid
And immovable buried in the soil.

The Fire Station

Outside the fire station, three engines are laid out
As though for airing. Just laid out in the sun,
Like linen, or tomatoes. They don't like confined spaces,
Fire engines, and can't be kept in the dark
For days on end. If there are no fires to attend
They need to be brought out into the air.
Just to breathe. Otherwise they might – I don't know –
Start lashing their tails, or butting their crimson
And silver heads against the doors. They might
Go mad. Who wouldn't? Looking down from
My apartment I watch the firemen, tiny
From this height, tend their engines. I feel
Their pride. They are cleaning them now,
And the engines drip and sparkle. And slowly dry.

Bridespotting

Along the waterfront, brides in drifts of white or red
As though they have blown in on a marriage wind.
Sometimes you find them in parks, on a path
Beneath pipes of bamboo, or on the shores of
Boating lakes, or on the old bridge that was once
The front line of an invading army. They form queues,
Sometimes stand on boxes concealed within their hulls
Of flowing silk, or else just pose. They become something
To collect, a kind of hobby, like train or birdspotting.
They might bring good luck. In their red gowns they are
Like gifts, purses of money, birthday letters. When
They appear in white against the backdrop of water
And the towers of Pudong, the older people must wonder
How they can still dazzle in their funeral colours.

Air-Con

I still don't understand it, even though I have come
To rely on its artificial breeze, and can only think
That somehow it draws air in from the outside
World and through a kind of refrigeration process
Cools it down and allows it to feed into the
Existing air of my room. Being cooler, it trickles
Down to the floor and builds from there. It makes
A noise that is a low and constant hum, like the noise
Of the city itself, and sometimes I have to leave it on
All night, moving in and out of sleep, in and out
Of its sound. Soon I'm as conscious of it as I am
Of the noise of my own existence, which is to say,
Hardly at all. Though in the reluctance to turn it off
There is that same wonder at what I'll hear in its absence.

Beggars

Supine, creaturely, abbreviated, they work,
And are in motion, continually. Are they brothers?
Old friends? One is on a makeshift bed that the other
Pushes like an old-style costermonger. Music
Plays achingly — dying violins, amplified, the speaker
Coddled in the bedclothes like a hot water bottle.
Is it *La Bohème* they are playing? The scene
Should be enacted in a closet or chamber,
But is out here, among the malls. Another one
Is solitary, someone I took at first to be an injured
Dog dragging itself by its forelimbs, until I saw
That it cast a tin along the pavement before it, which
It would follow, a torso on wheels. The tin moving
across the concrete, seemed to tear it open like paper.

Natural History

These fish fossils seem as remote from fish
As if someone had just written the word 'fish'
In water on dry cement. They have left of themselves
Little more than brief directional arrows caught
In the clothing of time. Each barely an inch
Long, a stroke of curled backbone, traces of fin
And scales, profile faces, featureless. Little menaces.
Though there is a strange sense of movement,
The rhythm of a million-year dance, the pattern
You might see in wallpaper or curtains, or written
Music. The fish repeat themselves, a strip
Of movie frames, fish montage. They've written down
Instructions for the dance. One step, an arrow
Another step, together, forwards, daa – da – da.

In Yu Garden

All the old town's carp have joined their dots
And formed a single, many-headed animal.
They blow bubbles of glass or gape and gasp in a corner
Of the pond, where the people pause on the stone
Walkway and stare as they might have stared once
Into the flames of a hearthfire. A girl crouches down
And reaches out as if to pick a fruit
From a bowl of living tangerines. What
Does she see in that toothless O that makes her want to
Use her pointing finger, that she might plug
The singing voice that could flow from that rosy throat,
To praise her other-worldliness, or is she
Picking one amongst the many who sees her
In the very act of being seen?

The Park

In Gucheng Park, there are forests of bamboo,
With paths that cut a series of lines through them.
On one of these paths there is an elderly lady.
She is walking slowly backwards. She cannot see
Where she is going. Her arms swing alternately
To rest on her stomach and the small of her back.
And she is singing as she walks backwards, beautifully.
I am at a junction and she is on the path
I need to take, filling it with her frail mirror body.
I hesitate. Just for a second. And then I am on her path
Through the bamboo. We are the only ones there
In bamboo shade. And she sings and I sing
Silently, and we walk together, backwards, forwards
For the time it takes for me to pass her.

The Buildings

The buildings are awake and have started moving around
And I am walking among them like an incognito
God. They have grown to love the world
And to know its ways. Their feet are clay.
I am awake and have started moving around.
The buildings move through me as though I breathed them.
Our feet are combed into the bedrock of the island.
My blinds are drawn. No one should live this way.
We are awake and have started moving around
The buildings are amazed and watch us blindly.
Through falls of windows we rise without leaving the ground
The sun itself has become a kind of wall
Though from the top we can see further than ever before
Buildings all around, almost as tall and standing still.

The Bronzes

They knew, who made these things, how to drink.
How a cup for wine could never stand on one
Leg, but needed three, and yet could still
Be on tip toes like ballerinas in Father
Christmas suits. Hammock-slung bellies and bulging thighs.
Only they would know the handle of a cup
Can become a squirming dragon in your hand
Or that a bat or tiger could breach the lip and peer
From the far rim across the quaking spirit,
Or how the warring states might find common ground
In a dream of horned cattle grazing a flagon's lid,
Horns locked and lost, their sacred muzzles dripping
With blood. Or those grooved and engraved faces,
That stare back at you when you take a sip.

The Lift

The lift is full, and the next one is stopping at every floor.
I am waiting with an elderly couple no bigger than children,
So decide to take the stairs eleven floors down. They are
Dimly lit, grubby concrete flights that lead
Down, one after another, deeper and deeper down
Into the earth (it feels), though I am really up
in the air, high up in the air coming
Down to earth. After floor 6 there are
No more doors off, but for small locked ones.
No more landings, but the stairs go down and down.
Then a flight in total darkness but for a green
Emergency light. I have no choice but to go deeper
Into the building – junk, rubbish, and then a door
Ajar and a happy radio beyond. I climb back up.

The Sirens

Should I worry when I hear the sirens?
I can see from the window the city carrying on
In its usual way, and in between a dozen
High-rises a vague, grey horizon where nothing
Is on fire. But the sirens call again.
Is it a flood? Has it really rained
That much? Was it only yesterday
Someone knocked and softly delivered
Two fire extinguishers, little
Toy soldiers that stand, a pair, by the couch?
The sirens exercise their right to be heard.
The traffic, mostly two-wheeled, moves at a pace
In time with the normal daily flow of things.
But still the sirens call. All morning they call.

The Cleaner

If she's invisible, it's not of my doing
Because I see her, and I hear her as well
Even though she does her thing quietly,
Making the bed with just a few turns
Of the clothes, wiping the floor with a silent brush,
Drying it with the same, though its gloss
Hardly needs cleaning. She works around me, as if
She was something I'd thought. But she's real
When she asks me what to do about
The thirty Shanghai Dailies that have been slipped
Under the door. Or when she does the bathroom,
Rearranging my pills and choked up razors, sponging
The shower door and giving a little gasp of surprise,
That stays with me for the rest of the day.

The Key Rings

Out of all these things – the deep-fried hairy crabs
In all their ginger seriousness, the views
Of silken mountains and monkeys, the blood-blister
Lanterns, the ware, the hair, the fans and scent
The whole trees of polymerized blossom, the ice-cream
Cones jewelled and bedecked and appended
So much they look like gadgets rather than food,
It is the key rings I most desire, that are
Perfect bowls of soup or stir fries, dumplings
In liquor, (one on the spoon), arrays of pak choi
Or a fish head, white beans, noodles, the whole
Caboodle hanging on the end of a little chain.
If you could shrink the world down to the size
Of a button, it could hardly be more surprising.

Sunflour

Their indifference has its own kind of charm.
Perhaps they have seen how I handle their cakes
Sometimes putting a fingertip to green icing
When the plastic tongs have proved inadequate.
Theirs are the sort I might bake from a recipe
Found in a dream, of a muffin accessorized
With Oreos like cufflinks studding its crust,
A fractal Danish infinitely repeating its cherry heart.
They are under glass, like museum pieces
Or instruments for a playful form of surgery.
The women are sterilized and masked
And surprised when I present cash, give call
And response, military-style cries from the floor.
It's just a bakery, I tell myself. It's just cakes.

The Unattended Bride

Someone has discarded a bride on the steps of the hotel.
She doesn't move and so I wonder if she's real.
It's strange to see an unattended bride,
But there is no one anywhere near, and the houses
Around about are the sort that look unlived in.
Seeing a bride alone makes you wonder if you can trust
What you see – brides don't just stand there,
In full dress and veil, flowered-up, on the steps,
Not moving, but that is what she does, (if that is doing something).
Who is going to check on her? See if she's breathing?
Look again, nothing here seems quite right.
This could be a film set, the gardens look English
Except for the banana trees. Slowly the bride
Turns her head and takes it all in.

The Malls

In places like this, my foreignness disappears
Along with everything else. These are my likenesses
In everything but dress, and likeness; window-still
Fibreglass Europeans clothed in Louis Vuitton.
I am carried aloft by the slow shuffle of a moving
Staircase, as though caught on a bridal train, or a garment
Raised from the dead. And each new floor is a version
Of the afterlife, shops on top of shops, an entire
Store given over to the display of one
Transcendental handbag. Who buys this stuff?
No one I have ever seen. She says
They are really warehouses, not shops. Shoes on plinths
In prim pairs, spotlit. Dolce and Gabbana.
I could live here for ever and ever and ever and ever.

The Ancient Villages

Everything works in the ancient villages – the lights
In the bathroom, the hot water, the throats of the birds who wake me
With songs I've never heard before. Drongos
And orioles, a flowerpecker? I don't know. I think of the train
That brought me here, so smooth it seemed the landscape
Moved instead. Its guards were militaristic,
And slept the whole journey heads back, mouths open,
Gaping throats exposed. Our guide told us
To follow his head, which was shaved and lantern bright.
The villages, he said, have brains, horns, intestines . . .
They are water buffaloes. In lulls he worked a chest-expander,
Vertically, with his foot but lost heart by the end of the tour,
We'd find him sitting on low walls by millponds, smoking,
Head hanging, his megaphone snoring beside him.

Museum

We come from a past that is small and perfectly formed
This is how it was, this is how we were
Our hair is lifelike, our skin is almost touchable
What can you say about us, what is there to say?
You'll find us crushed in the silk of an opium den
Or bent over a table of warring crickets
You can think of us, think of then, when this was
Feel nostalgia for a time you didn't know
For the candy-bright opera houses and music halls
Where we danced in silence and drank air
How did we get from there to here?
What have we been left with, or without?
We have been living here for ever, holding a candle
To the past. This is how we are. This is how it is.

Games

Among the things that people do in the park,
Is play this unfathomable game;
The elders bent over squared boards, thinking,
As if willing the pieces on to move by themselves.
I can see their minds are full of movement, dancing
Together, or in battle, but silently, and still.
I think of Borges's immortals who, beyond
The reach of death, find life a tiresome process
Of infinite stillness, and seeing no reason
To do anything else, stay where they have fallen.
There are no younger students of the game.
Nearby, the badminton players play without nets
As if chasing a feathered heart through the trees
That continues beating even when it falls.

Chefs

A glimpse of chefs through an open door at the back,
Of the restaurant. Four Chefs in all, at rest, looking nervous
As though backstage and trying to remember their lines.
They are four chefs in a passageway, shrunken successively
By perspective so the furthest chef could be a doll-chef
Seated in the nearest's lap, and played with,
If she had the strength to play. They are cartoon chefs,
In whites with chessboard trousers, mushroom-cloud
Hats, though they are energy converted to matter.
They sit, utterly spent, they don't talk, it's as though they are
Trying to find the recipe for themselves, and read it
In the damp carpet. They are each their own idea
Of a chef. It must have been in another world
They'd cooked, where there was joy in what they'd made.

English Corner

I talk with a retired chemical engineer
Whose daughter – his only child (sad face)
Allows him to live in her flat while she's away.
She is a travelling rep for a chemical company,
But she likes to sing. Really, she's a singer.
His wife? She teaches in a kindergarten
Or did until last year. But she also sings.
That's where his daughter gets her love of song.
It runs in the family. His brother sings in the opera
And is actually quite famous, but he, the man
I'm talking to, can't sing. He can only listen.
Sometimes, he says, he flies a kite. In the far
Corner of the park we can see the kite flyers
Tugging at the sky. I imagine they are his friends.

Autumn Ritual

The cart is loaded with its red sacks of hope,
The giant god of origami is wheeled into position,
And paper people rise on sticks above
The pillars of smoke, until a fire is lit
In the valence round the bed, and starts to climb
Like a dry thought quickly through the colours
Just as a song burns through the crowds.
Spires of heat and light, the material thing
Is gas, and elements of grey ash which tumble
Upwards to land like leaves from the trees on your clothes
And hair. The wonderful procession is now an echo
Of itself, its loveliness contained in this mute implosion
Weakened by its own energy. The stars find new
Distances and then slowly disappear.

The Pencil

for Yaxin

A pencil, 3B, unsharpened (unused), blue
With a black tip, a white collar and lettering
In gold, sits under glass beside a sheet
Of blank paper. Also in the cabinet —
Mao's hat, and his trousers, neatly folded.
Mao memorabilia, speeches, photos, happy
Porcelain Maos waving, but it is the pencil
That draws and holds my attention. A gift
To his calligrapher, I later learn, and returned
As a donation to the house where he'd lived.
I have worn my own pencils down to their roots
Some hardly bigger now than thumb tacks.
A shikumen house, waxworks, his bed, his chair,
But it is still the pencil that holds my attention.

The Walk

To plan a walk in a city so poorly mapped
Is like charting a journey across wild terrain,
I rely on memory and landmarks — a park here,
A flying saucer there, known ways, familiar buildings
I navigate an artery of my own thoughts,
Nanjing Road and Tomorrow Square, Julu,
Fughou, now they strain to retain their strangeness.
The old city's cables are bundles of nerves, I am
In the brain of the past, then watching the trees
Darken above Tianzifang and seeking consolation
In trinkets. I have walked far enough to meet people
I used to know, as though I'd had a childhood here.
Or that I had closed a loop in time, and the city
Had started to remember me, to map me.

The Horse

What if this horse I'm leading is in constant pain
How would I know, how could he ever tell me?
Walking the lanes back from the coast or crossing
The rocky plains he seemed to take it all
In his stride, even when my own feet
Were killing me, but then I noticed something
About the way he moved on smoother ground
Lifting his hooves like he'd stepped on something hot
While I myself trod a colder path.
I pictured him walking through fields of orange flame
Which to me were lawns of cool grass.
And nothing in his face betrayed the agony he felt
Until we came to rest beneath some trees
And in their shade he found the strength to speak.

ACKNOWLEDGEMENTS

'The Piano Tuner's Cough' first appeared in *PNReview*.

I would like to thank the Shanghai Writers' Association for their generosity during my two-month residency in their city in the autumn of 2019, during which a number of these poems were written. Thank you to Peihua and Haiyan especially.